EMPTY JARS

Also by Christopher Davis, Jr.

The Man Who Invented The Lawn Mower: And Other Inspirational Black Inventors And Their Inventions

The Woman Who Invented Weaving

Black Made That Collection Activity Book

Good Morning Matty!

The Novice Designer's Resource Guide: First Edition

EMPTY JARS

*The Keys To Overcoming Debt & Building Residual Wealth,
Using **The Elisha Method**™*

By: Christopher Davis, Jr.
Foreword By: Tamika L. Sims, Best-selling & Award-winning Author, Author Coach, Chief Principal - Get Write With Tamika

Copyright © 2019 by Christopher Davis Jr.

All rights reserved. This book or any portion thereof may not be reproduced or used in any manner whatsoever without the express written permission of the publisher except for the use of brief quotations in a book review.

Printed in the United States of America

First Printing, 2019

ISBN 9781093968132 (Paperback)

Edited By: Tamika L. Sims, Get Write with Tamika

Book Cover Design By: Christopher Davis, Jr., CRXWN Digital Media (www.CRXWNKulture.com)

Book Formatting By: Christopher Davis, Jr., CRXWN Digital Media (www.CRXWNKulture.com)

DEDICATION

I dedicate this book to every one of my mentors and friends in business that have helped me to nurture my entrepreneurial passion. I could not have made it this far without your guidance.

FOREWORD

When I was asked to originally write this Foreword, I immediately said yes because of my respect for Author Christopher Davis, Jr. What I did not realize is that this book would speak to me in a very real and profound way. I, like many of you, have found myself in a dry season, staring only at what was in front of me - lost, empty, broken and well, ready to die.

Just as we see in the case of this widow, all we have to do is look around and discover that the little oil we have, is the little oil that we need. In addition to the lessons of financial and wealth management, stewardship and obedience, I believe the greatest lesson hidden within the story is faith. I believe more than anything it is our faith that moves God. This widow's story proves that, especially, when she became faith in action.

Author Christopher Davis, Jr., has done an amazing job penning the lessons from this story and painting the picture of just how close our answers are if we would only dig deeper, be obedient and ask God for what we need. As a Christian entrepreneur, I have not always sought the Word of God - first. Consulting His Word last caused many things to go haywire in my business. While God always has the answer - He gives us free will. We have the power to make the choice - no matter what.

Now, I normally don't give advice, but here is a simple point of reference for you - take the lessons shared in this book seriously. Have pen and paper handy. Find a quiet place. Grab your Bible and study. Seek the wisdom of God as it pertains to your finances. Allow Him to give you the strategy to walk in the freedom you desire and deserve.

The recipe is simple - Author Christopher Davis Jr., has provided it for you, but this is only the beginning. You have to continue to ask, elevate your language and activate your faith. And then trust God to fill every empty jar you have.

Tamika L. Sims,
Best-selling & Award-winning Author, Author Coach, Chief Principal - Get Write With Tamika

TABLE OF CONTENTS

PREFACE	1
INTRODUCTION	7
1. SITUATIONS AND DRY SEASONS	9
2. A LITTLE BIT OF OIL	15
3. MIND YOUR OWN BUSINESS	23
4. ERASE YOUR DEBTS	31
5. RESIDUAL FLOW	37
CONCLUSION	41

PREFACE

*A*lthough I, personally identify as a Christian for my religious preference, the views expressed in this book are Biblically-based, but not solely applicable to those who believe in the Christian faith.

Anointed to be the great prophet Elijah's successor, the prophet Elisha was a force to be reckoned with. Elisha was not only a major prophet, but also a business consultant. This was another mantle that he wore during the course of his ministry. During one of Elisha's travels, he encountered a poor widow and her son. Her husband a prophet, the primary breadwinner of the family had died, and the family was in debt.

In her desperation and quest to find a solution, the woman goes to Elisha to help her with the debt situation before the creditor comes and takes her two sons away as slaves. The Prophet gives instructions that she needs to follow in dealing with her predicament.

As a Christian entrepreneur that believes faith and business cannot be separated, the concept of starting a business and paying off debts became clear as I read and meditated on the story of Elisha and the poor widow. I discovered that the instructions the Prophet gave the widow, were great strategies that Christians can use to pay off debt and become successful entrepreneurs. I also found out that these Biblical strategies are not hard; anyone determined to be debt free can use them.

Knowing so many people including Christians that are struggling with debt, I was inspired to turn what I learned through reading the Word of God into a book. I desire to help others not only pay off their debts with the strategies that Elisha gave the widow, but to also start businesses that will sustain them even after they have finished clearing debts.

As someone that has been called to be a Christian Entrepreneur, I believe God has given me the mandate to share His Word in the marketplace. Entrepreneurs in the marketplace should not be ashamed of preaching the Word of God and doing businesses built on Christian values. The marketplace needs more Christians that will be able to let their light shine so that customers and other business owners can see their good deeds and glorify God. Today, there is a need for more Christian influencers in the marketplace.

This practical book is for Christians looking for ways of paying off their debts and are ready to put into practice what they have learned. This book helps readers see that living in debt is not good. Debts make people live in a cycle of defeat and slavery. Approximately 7 out of every 10 Americans believe that "debt is a necessity in their lives", and approximately 8 out of every 10 Americans actually have debt right now. Most of us like to think that "someday" we will get out of the hole and quit being debt slaves, but very few of us ever actually accomplish this. That is because the entire system is designed to trap us in debt before we even get out into the "real world" and keep us in debt until we die. Sadly, most don't even realize what is being done to them. The Bible says that a borrower is a slave to the lender. Moving forward with life becomes challenging when you have a lot of debts. Unless one is willing to take action, you will continue getting into more debts. Paying off debts is not an easy thing, but it requires making sacrifices as explained in the book.

I am also writing for the Christian that wants to build their businesses on the right foundation. The Bible helps us spiritually, and it also covers all areas of our lives including entrepreneurship. As you read the practical steps and strategies that I have shared in this book, I hope a fire will be ignited in your heart to find something that you are passionate about and turn it into a business.

It is easy to start a business today and make money as explained in this book; all you need is faith, passion, and determination. Although the main story is about paying off debts, the challenges given at the end of each chapter are strategies that you can use to start up your own business even if you are not in debt.

Every chapter of this book goes deeply into a different verse or part of the story of the widow and from each verse that I have shared in the book, different solutions and strategies are laid down for the reader. Christian entrepreneurs can model this book when seeking guidance from the Word of God. There are many kinds of pieces of advice out there, some are good and others are not. But as Christians, we know that ultimately God's Word remains to be true, our only truth. Just the way the story of the widow is a good business model for Christian entrepreneurs that want to start their businesses, Scriptures can be used to find solutions to different challenges that entrepreneurs face.

INTRODUCTION

From the desk of Christopher Davis, Jr.

Like most Americans, my 12 years in school left me grossly unprepared financially for what was to come. I had no education on how to build my credit, the importance of my credit, or the effect that taking on student loans and credit cards debts would have long-term. Within that first year of me being in college, I managed to acquire almost $20,000 in debt between student loans and credit cards. Like the main character of this book, I was in deeper debt than I could manage. None of my three jobs that I was working at the time paid enough to afford my cost of living and my debts.

It didn't take long for me to realize that I had become stuck in a vicious cycle of debt to income ratio. I wasn't making enough on my minimum wage jobs to cover my debts acquired through school. Completing my degree meant acquiring more debt, and all of my good-paying job prospects required a degree. I felt as if there was no way I'd ever be free of the burden.

Fast forward 10 years later, I wrote and self-published my first book. At the time, I understood very little about the power of residual income and how it could impact my life. It had been on my heart to do it, therefore I did. Three months later, I received my first publishing royalty check. Surprisingly, it was enough to cover my monthly debt payments that were in default at the time. I used the money to catch up on the payments, and setup auto-debit the day after my royalties deposited each month.

The point I'm making is, I found a way to use the gifts and talents that I had to create the extra income needed to repay my debts, and using The Elisha Method™. As you continue to read this book, I will show you how to do the same.

1

SITUATIONS AND DRY SEASONS

"One day the widow of a member of the group of prophets came to Elisha and cried out, "My husband who served you is dead, and you know how he feared the Lord. But now a creditor has come, threatening to take my two sons as slaves.""

2 Kings 4:1 NLT

Let's first understand the widow's situation. Her husband was presumably a major income contributor and primary provider in her household. Like most prophets during this time period, the woman's husband most likely did not profit very much from his service to the Lord, and was seemingly rationed enough for his family to survive on from the church. We may assume that the man had to borrow funds during some particularly hard times, which he did not repay before he died. During that time period, poverty was more commonly spread, and systems like welfare and food stamps did not exist. At the least, we could say that she and her family's basic needs were met when her husband was alive.

They probably managed to save up very little, but still had enough in savings to take care of the woman and her two sons for the brief time period between when her husband died, and when the woman encountered Elisha. Most of the details of this story are left to the imagination to be pieced together by context clues, however the one undisputed fact remains; the woman was in her dry season.

In ancient Israel, when a debt was owed, family members could be taken as slaves to work off the debt, this was today's equivalent of working a dead-end job for a boss who mistreats you and does not value you just to repay your loans. The woman feared that her husband's creditor would soon return to collect and her sons would be the payment for her deceased husband's debts.

Like any good mother, she would have done anything to protect her family, but she didn't know where to start. So in a desperate attempt, she reached out to one of the prophets that belonged to the same group that her husband used to, named Elisha...hoping that because of the former relationship that he and the husband had, that he could loan her the money to repay the debts. The problem with this line of thinking is that she would always be in debt; simply moving the debt from one creditor to the next every time it was time to repay.

How many of us can identify with the widow's situation? How many of us have excessive debts or have ever had excessive debts? How many of us live paycheck to paycheck, and are just barely scraping by? How many of us have let the fear of losing all that we have control over in our lives and critically impact our rational thinking? **The dry seasons in our lives can drive us to do things that only bring about temporary relief, like**

getting a title loan to catch up on bills. These decisions trap you in an endless cycle of always being the borrower, until you eventually run out of sources to borrow from.

Chapter Challenge: STOP FEEDING THE CYCLE

If you are reading this and you are in your financial dry season, reflect on what behaviors that you have been partaking in that are feeding the cycle. Are you, as they say, robbing Peter to pay Paul? Maybe you have been paying your bills with credit cards or refinancing loans to pay off other loans; or maybe you are stretching your finances thinner than you should for reasons that you should not. Whatever your situation is, write down all of the ways that you have been causing your own financial dry seasons, and at the bottom of the paper, in all capital letters, write THIS ENDS TODAY! Post it somewhere that you will see it daily and make a conscious decision to not return to those destructive patterns ever again.

EMPTY JARS

WHAT IS CAUSING MY DRY SEASON?

CHRISTOPHER DAVIS, JR.

_____
_____
_____
_____
_____
_____
_____

THIS ENDS TODAY!!!

2

A LITTLE BIT OF OIL

""What can I do to help you?" Elisha asked. "Tell me, what do you have in the house?" "Nothing at all, except a flask of olive oil," she replied."

2 Kings 4:2 NLT

Realizing the gravity of her situation, the widow pursues help the only way that she knows how. Who knows what thoughts ran through her head as she asked Elisha for help. I'd guess it was the equivalent of meeting with the bank's loan officer for a loan, knowing that your credit is bad and that you have no collateral. It was probably one of the most nerve-wrecking experiences, and it could not have been very easy for her to present her case.

Elisha's response to the widow's request was not at all what she expected and caught her off guard. Rather than telling her what funds he had that could have been used to help her, he asked the woman what *she* had in her house. Her response was probably driven by the instinctive thought that Elisha had an ulterior motive.

Maybe he was asking to see if she had anything of value worth the money that she was asking for. Even though this was not the case, this is a pivotal point in the story. There were two parts to her response that give insight into how she viewed her situation:

Part (1): "Nothing at all" - This is how most people view their dry seasons in life, as if they have nothing at all to offer; or they fear that the little they have will be stripped away. They often don't realize that God can do so much with so little, but He requires faith. Faith in essence is a mindset shift. **The difference between a wealthy mindset and the poor mindset is the poor will see a blank page as it is...blank. A wealthy mindset sees a blank page as a canvas to be filled with the next million dollar idea.**

Part (2): "except a flask of olive oil" - Now she was getting somewhere. She, in her poor mindset, just presented Elisha her metaphorical blank piece of paper. Thankfully Elisha did not share her same line of thinking. Where she saw, "nothing," he saw potential. God, through Elisha, was about to change her life by first changing the way that she thought and perceived her situation.

Olive oil at the time, and even in this present day and age, has many uses. It was needed for cooking, used for hair care, and highly regarded as a sacred symbol that the anointing of God rested on someone. These were only a few of the uses for olive oil that made it valued in the woman's culture. Though she didn't have much, the widow didn't realize the value in what she had.

She thought that her problem was not having enough money to repay the debt, when the real problem was that she did not realize that she'd already had everything that she needed to generate the income to change her financial outlook.

Chapter Challenge: SEEK OUT WISE COUNSEL

Thinking and doing are two different things. Stress has a way of clouding our judgments. When deep in debt we are mostly thinking of how to get out of it without really finding practical solutions to do that. We run around looking for quick solutions that do not necessarily help us to be debt free. Getting advice from an expert or a friend that is good in such matters is important because they are able to give us sound advice.

While we are likely to act on our emotions because of the challenges we are facing, the other person will be able to point out debt cancellation strategies that will work. They may not say what you want to hear, but listening and putting into practice what you learn will help you get out of a sticky situation.

Seek out a mentor, business consultant or business-savvy friend that can point you in the right direction. Write down what is discussed and formulate a complete idea for how your talents, gifts or skills can generate you constant income. Then pray on it, and ask God to show you the resources needed to bring your idea to life.

CHRISTOPHER DAVIS, JR.

WHO CAN GIVE ME WISE ADVICE CONCERNING MY BUSINESS & FINANCES?

EMPTY JARS

3

MIND YOUR OWN BUSINESS

"And Elisha said, "Borrow as many empty jars as you can from your friends and neighbors. Then go into your house with your sons and shut the door behind you. Pour olive oil from your flask into the jars, setting each one aside when it is filled." So she did as she was told. Her sons kept bringing jars to her, and she filled one after another. Soon every container was full to the brim! "Bring me another jar," she said to one of her sons. "There aren't any more!" he told her. And then the olive oil stopped flowing."

2 Kings 4:3-6 NLT

Elisha had unofficially become her Business Consultant, as reflected in the verse excerpt. His advice to her was to start a business using what she already had: olive oil. He instructed her to gather as many empty jars as possible even if she had to borrow them. Empty jars were regarded as worthless, and discarded just as easily, so finding people who would be willing to part with them wasn't the hard part. Asking for help from strangers could have proven to be a more difficult challenge.

Pride and fear aside, the woman realized the desperation of her situation and that if she did not do something, nothing would change. **Faith cannot yield results when there is no action to power it.** The widow didn't just wait on God to get her out of debt. She consulted with wise counsel, developed a plan and then acted on the plan.

I found it particularly interesting that Elisha told the woman to shut the door before she got started. This was symbolic and good advice for multiple reasons. The first being that only faith-filled people needed to be present for what was about to take place. Only a select few are privy to what God wants to accomplish through you, and there is no room for doubters or spectators.

EMPTY JARS

The woman and her sons believed, just as her husband did, in the miraculous power of The Most High God. For the miracle that God was about to perform, only those with strong faith would be able to interpret what was happening.

Secondly, shutting the door behind her would help her focus on filling the jars. It could be that the people she had borrowed these vessels from wanted to know what she was up to. If she had left her door open, they would have come to see what she was doing. By shutting the door, the widow was shutting off distractions.

The woman took the little oil and kept pouring until all the jars were filled. The supply did not run out, it only stopped when the last jar was full. It took faith on the part of the woman to take a jar of oil and start pouring on all the vessels. We do not know how long it took her to fill all the jars, but we don't see her taking a break from the task that she was doing. Apart from faith, we see a determined woman that is ready to do everything it takes to get out of debt. She did not get comfortable when things started looking up for her family.

Chapter Challenge: WHAT SKILL/PRODUCT DO YOU HAVE THAT IS BUSINESS-WORTHY?

What skill set or hidden talent do you possess that you could potentially monetize? How can your talents, gifts or skills benefit people? A few examples of professions that generate passive residual income are:

- Bloggers/Vloggers - bloggers and vloggers receive residual payments from paid advertising and product placement, merch sales and reviewing books, shows, movies and restaurants. Some of them offer services like writing content for other blogs, virtual assistant services, graphic design and coaching

- Authors - authors receive monthly/quarterly payments from online and physical book sales.

Find something that you are good at and use that to give value to clients at a fee. Step out on faith and always be faithful with the little that you have and see God open doors. Do not overlook the resources that you have because that is what God will use. Do not give up. It will not be easy especially when you are starting out. Creating quality products or finding something

something that you are passionate about and packaging it into a service is not easy, but, it will be worth it in the end.

Where are you spending most of your free time when you are not at work? Is it on social media, watching television, or spending it with friends who are always complaining and blaming everyone, but themselves about their money troubles? Distractions prevent people from being productive. You may say that you do not have enough time to go to work and do business on the side, but there also people out there who go to work and run successful businesses. They have the same hours like you, but have found a way of balancing life. Shut off everything that is stealing away your time and like the widow, work hard until you achieve the results that you want.

Please note that this chapter of the book mildly discusses converting your hobbies & skills into a lucrative business. For more information concerning how to accomplish this, purchase the second book in the installment, titled, "What's In Your Hand?: How To Go From Underemployed To Self-Employed & Never Look Back, Using The Moses Method™."

CHRISTOPHER DAVIS, JR.

WHAT SKILL(S) DO I HAVE THAT I COULD MONETIZE?

EMPTY JARS

4

ERASE YOUR DEBTS

*"When she told the man of God what had happened, he said to her, "Now sell the olive oil and **pay your debts**, and you and your sons can live on what is left over.""*

2 Kings 4:7 NLT

Isn't it great that after the jars were full, the woman went back to the prophet for the next set of instructions? Maybe if it was another person, they would have called up for a family meeting and strategized on the next set of actions, after all the Prophet had already given them a great strategy. But the woman was determined to see this to the end and what better way for her to do it, than to go back to the prophet for more guidance.

The FIRST thing the woman was instructed to do was pay her debt; freeing herself from the cause of her dry seasons.

Paying off debt first meant that the widow would have to deny her family some things for some time. Given that the creditor was coming for her sons, it means that they were living in abject poverty. They barely had anything. But, depending on the amount of debt they had, they would have to continue living the same way even if they were making a lot of money from their business. She needed to have the right priorities with the money that was coming in from her business so that she could be free from her debtors. The woman had to stick to the plan that was presented to her by the prophet or she would never achieve her goals.

What if the prophet had told her to first cover basic needs, then pay off the debt? Would they have paid off the creditor eventually? Well, we are not told if she went through with the plan, but given that she was obedient up to this point, we believe that she followed the instructions the Prophet gave her. Was it easy for her? I don't think so, but the fact that her sons were going to be slaves may have kept her in check.

It is possible for someone to make a lot of money and still continue living in debt. **When your priorities are wrong, clearing debts becomes a challenge.** In fact, if you asked around, you will find that though some people are earning more money now than when they started out, they have more debts than when they were earning little money. Why? The more they earn, the more they spend and the more they borrow loans.

Chapter Challenge: WIPE THE SLATE CLEAN

It's time to set the right priorities. Write down the amount of debt that you have and then start paying it off. How you clear the debt will depend on the amount you owe and how much you are making. If the debt is small, then get the money and pay all of it. But if you have different loans break them down into small amounts and start paying them off either on a monthly or weekly basis depending on how you make money. When your business starts producing income make sure to clear your debts first, even if it requires setting up payment plans. Make it a point to clear your debt and stay out of any other kind of debt in future.

WHO DO I OWE?

Company Name: _____

Amount Owed: $_____

Company Name: _____

Amount Owed: $_____

Company Name: _____

Amount Owed: $_____

Company Name: _____

Amount Owed: $_____

Company Name: _____

Amount Owed: $_____

Company Name: _____

Amount Owed: $_____

Company Name: _____

CHRISTOPHER DAVIS, JR.

Amount Owed: $_____

Company Name: _____

Amount Owed: $_____

Company Name: _____

Amount Owed: $_____

Company Name: _____

Amount Owed: $_____

Company Name: _____

Amount Owed: $_____

Company Name: _____

Amount Owed: $_____

Company Name: _____

Amount Owed: $_____

5
RESIDUAL FLOW

*"When she told the man of God what had happened, he said to her, "Now sell the olive oil and pay your debts, and you and your sons can **live on what is left over.**""*

2 Kings 4:7 NLT

Elisha told the woman to live off what was left. We do not know how much she owed; neither do we know how many jars hers sons borrowed. But, the amount of money she was going to be left with after paying the debt was dependent on how many jars she filled. It means that if her sons did not borrow enough jars, the woman would only pay off her creditors, then the family would continue living in poverty and maybe it could only be a matter of time before she was in debt again.

But, if she borrowed enough jars then she had a lot of oil that she could sell and get money to clear her debts, take care of her family, invest and even save. God met her need, but He gave her a chance to act on her faith by not telling her the exact number of vessels she needed. Of course God is all knowing, so He knew the exact number of jars that the woman needed, but the Prophet told her borrow as many empty jars as possible. She was given a chance to decide how much she wanted, meaning that God was not going to limit her because He is able to do exceedingly, abundantly and above all, that we could ask or think.

EMPTY JARS

God was not offering this widow a temporary solution, He wanted to give her much more than she needed, so that she could live a life of abundance. But she needed to play her part of being faithful and obedient.

Another thing that the prophet did not tell her was how much she should charge her customers. So, she had to come up with a pricing strategy that would help her sell the oil to make enough money. She also had to look for customers, Elisha did not tell her to go back home, sit and wait for customers to come and buy her product. In order to sell the oil, she would have to actively look for customers that were interested in her product.

All through this story, we see that the woman needed to act on her faith. She was collaborating with God to cancel her debt. Even when what the prophet told her sounded ridiculous it did not stop her from obeying. She was diligent and did not tire until all the jars were full and later went back to the Prophet for the next set of instructions.

Chapter Challenge: RIDE THE RESIDUAL WAVE

The amount of money you are going to be left with after your debt is paid off will depend on how much effort you are willing to put in. Paying off debt is not easy because you will have to forego some things. You will have to cut down on your expenses and that means cutting down on things that you love or make you comfortable.

Now that your debts have been taken care of, you have to learn how to stay out of debt or you will be back to the same cycle. Allow your residual income to build by having multiple sources. Save money. Invest in assets. Simply stated, assets are those things that will bring you money.

It is not enough to clear your debt and save money in the bank, make sure you invest in some assets so that you can always have money coming in.

CONCLUSION

Writing this book has taught me that the best entrepreneurship lessons and instructions are in the Word of God. I have learned how to turn the Bible into an instructional book for my business. There is a lot that we can learn and apply to our business when we do things God's way.

The version adopted in this book is the New Living Translation. I have shared the story from different angles according to the revelations that I got while reading it so that it can be easy for the reader to relate their life to the story. While the story happened a long time ago, the concepts still apply today, in the book I have made comparisons of some of those concepts with the things that people go through today so that you can see how this story applies to us today.

I encourage you to step out on faith like the widow and take up necessary actions. Do not create excuses or postpone taking up challenges. Find accountability partners that will help you in this journey of paying debts and starting your own business.

As you read through the book, I would urge you to ask God to help you understand the concepts that have been laid down. Ask Him to reveal to you more concerning your business. Let Him show you how to go about your business and debt situation because He knows the best way for you to deal with what you are going through. In the Old Testament, people had to go to prophets for guidance, but now we have direct access to God through his son Jesus.

Allow God to speak to you through this book and the Bible about your business and life. Just like the way the widow dealt with her issue because she listened to God, listen to what God is telling you and then trust and obey Him.

ABOUT THE AUTHOR

- Christopher Davis, Jr. -

Christopher Davis Jr, of CRXWN Digital Media, has been instrumental in the development and success of several small businesses over time. Specialized in building marketable and sustainable business brands for small businesses, he has a natural acumen for improving the structure, productivity, and profitability of any business. Christopher Davis Jr. has been in the design and marketing industry for over a decade and a half now. He has worked with clients from all parts of the world and built a reputable business front with a digital presence on a global scale.

Christopher is also the Owner of the all-natural hair and skin care product line, CRXWN All-Natural Products; which is currently being sold in local stores and barbershops in the U.S. and Germany.

Before becoming a full-fledged business owner and growing in the full spectrum of entrepreneurship, Christopher has always been business savvy, with a Midas touch, turning all he touches to gold. From selling candy to mowing lawns to selling drawings and sketches to his classmates, he has always carried that unrivaled passion to do great and succeed in business.

He has authored several books, audio-books, and eBooks with 10 successfully trending titles, all of which were inspired by experiences in business, family, studies, and life as a whole. Through the many failures and triumphs, pitfalls and rising in business and in life, Christopher has learned the many secrets, principles, and guidelines to succeeding in business. This, his passion and his strong faith in God, has been handy in teaching and helping others in startups, building, sustenance and breaking even in their respective business ventures.

In addition to being a business consultant, an entrepreneur, and an author, Christopher is also a father to four wonderful sons and a husband to his beautiful wife. He enjoys outdoor recreational activities and traveling with his family.

www.ingramcontent.com/pod-product-compliance
Lightning Source LLC
Chambersburg PA
CBHW072254170526
45158CB00003BA/1070